Dear Reader,

We all need our own little BLUEPRINTS, or plans, in life. Sometimes making a plan is fun. Sometimes it's hard. Sometimes the plan doesn't work, so we make a new one. And sometimes, the plan is exactly what we need, just when we need it. As you read this Have a Plan Book, we hope you will ask questions, talk about it with family and friends, and create your very own plan. You can do this on your own or together with a grown-up.

Your plan may grow and change each time you read your book, and that's great! As life happens, plans change. But remember, having a little Blueprint is always helpful, in difficult times and in good times. So go ahead: BLUEPRINT IT!

Lovingly,

Your friends at little BLUEPRINT

P.S. Children and adults around the world are making their own little BLUEPRINTS. If you want to see the plans of others, or share yours, just go to

www.littleBLUEPRINT.com

HAVE A PLAN Books

To purchase a hardcover or
personalized version of any
little BLUEPRINT book,
with names, optional photo(s),
and details, please go to:

www.littleBLUEPRINT.com

The author would like to thank,
for all of their support and expertise:
Dan Siegel, M.D.;
Nina Shapiro, M.D.;
Lori Woodring, Phd. and Nan Miller, Phd.; and
my editors, Leslie Budnick and Gina Shaw.
A special thanks to Dignity Memorial;
Phoebe, age 10, for her blueprint illustration; and
Asher, age 7, for his title page illustration.

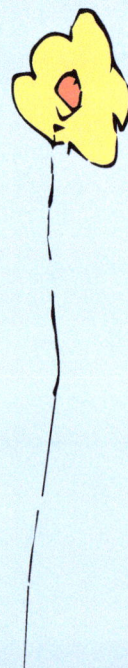

WHEN I MISS
My Special Pet,
I HAVE A PLAN

by Katherine Eskovitz

illustrated by Jessica Churchill

This is my special pet. I can draw or paste

a picture here to remember my

VERY SPECIAL PET.

I LOVE

my pet.

My pet died.

People and pets cannot die
because we think they will die,
or we say they will die,
or we act badly.

Dying happens because
the body stops working
and cannot be fixed.

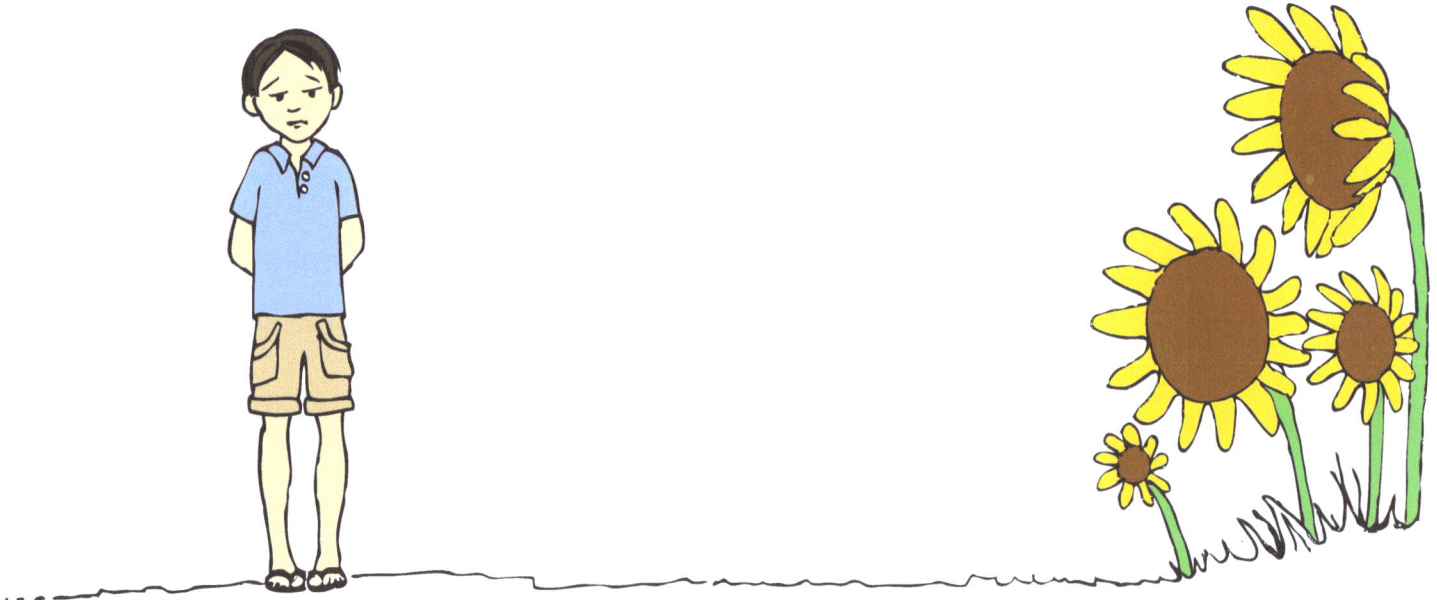

All living things have
A BEGINNING, A MIDDLE,
AND AN END.

MY PET
WILL NEVER BE ALIVE AGAIN.

When people and pets die, their heart stops
beating, and their brain stops working.

They do not breathe, think,
see, move, or feel.

Animals

die because they are very, very, very old; or very, very, very ill; or they get into a very, very, very bad accident.

I miss my pet

SO MUCH.

One way we say good-bye is to have a funeral.

A FUNERAL IS A CEREMONY

where family and friends share their sadness

and their special memories.

Many people cry at a funeral because they are sad.

Every family has its own

THOUGHTS,

TRADITIONS,

AND BELIEFS

about death.

I can ask my parents about our family.

When a pet dies,
we mourn.

When we mourn, we think a lot about
our pet. We feel sad that we can no
longer see or be with our pet.
We cry if we feel like it.

Mourning

gives us the time we need to feel sad.

It takes time to feel better after a pet dies.

We all mourn in our own way.

We might TALK, CRY, LAUGH, or PLAY.

We can mourn alone and
together with family and friends.

We can comfort each other by
GIVING A HUG or TELLING A STORY.

Mourning is hard work.

IT MAKES ME TIRED.

I have lots of emotions. I feel sad, I feel angry,

and sometimes I feel nothing at all.

I want to see my pet again,

but I know I can't.

When I am feeling sad,
I can do things to remember
happy times we spent together.
I can draw a picture.

I can talk to my parents
and friends about how I feel.
I can ask them questions.

I can make an

ALBUM,

A MEMORY BOOK,

OR A KEEPSAKE BOX

for pictures, cards, and notes.

I can keep something that belonged to my special pet
IN A SAFE PLACE.

I CAN NAME A STUFFED ANIMAL

after my pet.

I CAN PLANT SOMETHING

in the garden in my pet's honor.

I can start by making

a plan of how to honor and remember

my special pet.

Here is MY PLAN

www.littleBLUEPRINT.com

Check out other children's BLUEPRINTS from around the world and share yours, too!

Other titles in the
HAVE A PLAN Series

WHEN IT'S TIME FOR BED, I HAVE A PLAN

TO CELEBRATE THE HOLIDAYS, I HAVE A PLAN

TO BE A HEALTHY EATER, I HAVE A PLAN

WHEN I MISS SOMEONE SPECIAL, I HAVE A PLAN

TO BE SAFE AT HOME, I HAVE A PLAN

TO BE SAFE ON THE GO, I HAVE A PLAN

TO KEEP MY BODY SAFE, I HAVE A PLAN

WHEN MY PARENTS DIVORCE, I HAVE A PLAN

WHEN MY PARENTS SEPARATE, I HAVE A PLAN

AND MORE

New titles added regularly at
www.littleBLUEPRINT.com

All titles are available ready-made and personalized

playground

school

Home

little
BLUEPRINT
Empowering children. Training the brain.
WWW.LITTLEBLUEPRINT.COM

www.ingramcontent.com/pod-product-compliance
Lightning Source LLC
LaVergne TN
LVHW072101070426
835508LV00002B/213